MODULE 1:

Introduction to Coding Languages

Lesson 1: Introduction to Coding

What is coding?

- Coding is the process of using a programming language to instruct a computer to perform tasks. It involves writing commands that the machine can interpret and execute.
- From websites to mobile apps, operating systems to AI, coding powers almost all aspects of modern technology.

Overview of Popular Coding Languages

- Python: Known for its readability and simplicity. It's widely used in web development, data science, artificial intelligence, and automation.
- JavaScript: Essential for front-end web development. It powers dynamic websites and enables interaction with HTML and CSS.
- C++: A high-performance language often used in game development, systems software, and applications requiring direct hardware manipulation.
- Java: An object-oriented language widely used for building enterprise-scale applications, Android apps, and backend systems.
- Ruby: Another easy-to-learn language, especially known for its use in web development via the Ruby on Rails framework.

Setting Up a Development Environment

- Text Editors and IDEs: Introduce basic text editors (VS Code, Sublime Text) and more powerful integrated development environments (IDEs) like PyCharm, IntelliJ IDEA, and Visual Studio.
- Installing Required Software:
    - Install Python (for Python programming), Node.js (for JavaScript), and GCC (for C++).
    - Command line basics: Use the terminal to navigate directories, run scripts, and manage files.

Introduction to Programming Syntax and Structures

- Syntax: Every language has its syntax or set of rules that must be followed for the code to be understood by the machine. For instance, Python relies on indentation for structure, while JavaScript requires semicolons to end statements.
- Basic Structures: Overview of variables, loops, conditionals, and functions. These are fundamental components of any code and provide the logic flow and functionality to programs.

Lesson 2: Python Basics

Variables and Data Types

- Variables: Containers for storing data values. Example: `x = 5`, `name = "Alice"`.
- Data Types:
    - Primitive Types: Integers, floats, strings, booleans.
    - Complex Types: Lists, tuples, dictionaries.

Loops and Conditionals

- Loops:
    - For Loop: Iterating over a sequence. Example: `for i in range(10): print(i)`.
    - While Loop: Repeating an action as long as a condition holds true.
- Conditionals:
    - `if`, `elif`, `else`: Control the flow of the program based on conditions. Example: `if x > 5: print("x is greater than 5")`.

Functions and Modules

- Functions: Reusable blocks of code that perform a specific task. Example:
    ```python
    def greet(name):
        return f"Hello, {name}"
    ```

- Modules: Importing and using external libraries to extend functionality. Example: `import math` to use mathematical functions.

Basic Projects

- Calculator Project: Build a calculator that can perform basic arithmetic operations like addition, subtraction, multiplication, and division.
- Number Guessing Game: Create a game where the user must guess a randomly generated number. Use loops and conditionals to give feedback on whether the guesses are too high or low.

Lesson 3: JavaScript Fundamentals

Introduction to Front-End Development:

- Explanation of the relationship between HTML (structure), CSS (styling), and JavaScript (interaction). JavaScript allows for dynamic behavior like responding to user actions (e.g., clicks, typing) and updating the webpage content without reloading.

DOM Manipulation:

- DOM (Document Object Model): JavaScript interacts with the web page's structure using the DOM. You can change the structure, style, and content of HTML elements programmatically.
- Manipulating HTML:
    - Selecting elements: `document.getElementById("myElement")`.
    - Changing content: `element.innerHTML = "New content"`.
    - Modifying styles: `element.style.color = "blue"`.

Event Handling:

- Events: Learn how to handle user actions like clicks, key presses, and mouse movements. Example: `element.addEventListener("click", function() { ... })`.
- Example Project: A simple interactive webpage where users can add, edit, or remove items from a to-do list.

Lesson 4: Coding Best Practices

Writing Clean and Efficient Code:

- Code Readability: Follow naming conventions, use comments to explain complex sections, and break code into smaller, reusable functions.
- DRY Principle: Don't Repeat Yourself – avoid duplication by writing functions that can be reused.

Debugging Techniques and Tools:

- Print Debugging: Use print statements (or `console.log` in JavaScript) to track variables and outputs during program execution.
- Debugging Tools: Learn to use the built-in debuggers in VS Code, PyCharm, or browser DevTools to step through code and identify issues.
- Error Handling: Manage potential errors with try-except (Python) or try-catch (JavaScript).

Version Control with Git and GitHub:

- Git Basics: Learn how to initialize a repository, make commits, and create branches to manage different versions of code.
- GitHub Collaboration: Push code to GitHub, create pull requests for code reviews, and resolve conflicts in collaborative projects.

- Example Workflow: Work on a small collaborative project where each student works on a feature branch, pushes their changes, and merges into the main branch.

MODULE 2:

Introduction to Artificial Intelligence (AI)

Lesson 1: What is AI?

Definitions and Core Concepts of AI:

- Artificial Intelligence (AI): The ability of machines to perform tasks that typically require human intelligence, such as learning, problem-solving, and decision-making.
- Machine Learning (ML) vs. Artificial Intelligence: Machine learning is a subset of AI focused on the idea that machines can learn from data.
- Deep Learning (DL): A subset of machine learning involving neural networks with multiple layers, often used in image and speech recognition.

Types of AI:

- Narrow AI: AI that is designed to perform a narrow task (e.g., facial recognition, internet search engines). This is the most common type of AI today.
- General AI: AI that possesses human-level cognitive abilities across multiple domains. This remains theoretical and is not yet fully realized.
- Superintelligent AI: A hypothetical form of AI that surpasses human intelligence in all respects, including creativity, decision-making, and problem-solving.

Real-World Applications of AI:

- Natural Language Processing (NLP): AI systems like chatbots (e.g., Siri, Alexa) that can understand and generate human language.

- Computer Vision: AI used for object recognition, facial recognition, and image classification.
- AI in Healthcare: Diagnostic systems, personalized treatment plans, drug discovery.
- AI in Finance: Algorithmic trading, credit scoring, fraud detection.

The Future of AI:

- Explore the potential impact of AI on various industries, the economy, and society. Discuss both optimistic and cautious perspectives on AI's growth.

Lesson 2: Python for AI

Introduction to Python Libraries for AI:

- NumPy: A library for handling large, multi-dimensional arrays and matrices, along with a collection of mathematical functions to operate on these arrays.
- Pandas: A powerful data manipulation and analysis library. It offers data structures like DataFrames, making it easy to manage and analyze datasets.
- Matplotlib and Seaborn: Libraries for data visualization, useful for plotting graphs and charts to understand data patterns.

Introduction to Machine Learning Libraries:

- Scikit-Learn: A library that provides simple and efficient tools for data mining and data analysis. It is built on NumPy, SciPy, and matplotlib and offers various algorithms like linear regression, decision trees, k-nearest neighbors, and more.
- TensorFlow and Keras: Libraries used for building and training neural networks, particularly deep learning models. TensorFlow is more flexible but complex, while Keras offers a user-friendly interface for quick model development.

Introduction to Neural Networks:

- Basic Concepts: Learn about artificial neurons, layers, and how they connect to form neural networks.

- Feedforward Neural Networks: The simplest form of neural network, where data moves in only one direction (from input to output).
- Activation Functions: Functions such as ReLU (Rectified Linear Unit) and Sigmoid, which help the network learn complex patterns by introducing non-linearity.
- Training and Backpropagation: Understand how neural networks learn by adjusting weights through an algorithm called backpropagation, which minimizes the error (loss) of the network.

Hands-on Practice:

- Practice with Libraries: Work on small exercises using NumPy, Pandas, and Scikit-Learn to manipulate data and create simple machine learning models.

Lesson 3: Building Your First AI Model

Data Processing for AI:

- Data Cleaning: Handle missing data, outliers, and erroneous entries. Learn the importance of data quality in AI.
- Feature Selection: Identify relevant features (input variables) that will improve model accuracy.
- Data Normalization: Standardize or normalize data to ensure all features have the same scale, which is crucial for certain AI algorithms.

Building an AI Model:

- Choosing a Dataset: Select a simple dataset (e.g., MNIST for image classification, Titanic survival for binary classification).
- Model Architecture: Define the layers, number of neurons, activation functions, and output layer based on the type of task (classification or regression).
- Model Training: Use backpropagation and gradient descent to train the model by minimizing the error or loss function.

Evaluating AI Models:

- Metrics for Classification**: Accuracy, precision, recall, F1-score, confusion matrix. Learn how to interpret these metrics to assess model performance.
- Metrics for Regression**: Mean Absolute Error (MAE), Mean Squared Error (MSE), R-squared.
- Validation and Testing**: Split the dataset into training, validation, and test sets to ensure the model generalizes well to unseen data.

Hands-on Project:

- Image Recognition Project: Build a simple AI model for image recognition using the MNIST dataset. Train the model to recognize hand-written digits and evaluate its performance on test data.

Lesson 4: Ethical Considerations in AI

AI Bias And Fairness:

- What is AI?: Explore how biased training data can lead to biased AI models. Examples of bias in AI include facial recognition systems that perform poorly on people with darker skin tones due to a lack of diverse training data.
- Ensuring Fairness: Techniques to mitigate bias, including collecting diverse data, using fairness-aware algorithms, and monitoring model outputs for biased decisions.

Privacy and Security Concerns:

- Data Privacy: AI often relies on massive amounts of personal data, raising concerns about privacy and data ownership. Discuss how to protect user data and comply with regulations like GDPR.
- Security in AI Systems: Explore vulnerabilities in AI systems, such as adversarial attacks, where small, imperceptible changes to input data can trick AI models into making wrong predictions.

Responsible AI:

- Transparency and Explainability: Emphasize the importance of creating AI systems whose decision-

making processes can be understood by humans. Discuss methods for explaining AI decisions, such as SHAP values and LIME (Local Interpretable Model-agnostic Explanations).
- AI Accountability: Define who is responsible when AI systems fail or make harmful decisions, and the importance of having clear guidelines for AI developers and users.

Best Practices for Ethical AI:

- Establishing Ethical Guidelines: Encourage companies and developers to establish ethical guidelines for AI development. Review existing ethical frameworks from organizations like the Partnership on AI.
- Building Fair and Transparent Models: Incorporate bias mitigation techniques, data privacy practices, and explainability into the AI development process from the outset.

MODULE 3

Machine Learning

Lesson 1: Machine Learning Basics

Introduction to Machine Learning (ML):

- What is Machine Learning?: Machine learning is the process of training machines to recognize patterns and make decisions based on data without being explicitly programmed for specific tasks.
- Supervised Learning vs. Unsupervised Learning
  - Supervised Learning: Models learn from labeled data. Examples include classification (e.g., spam detection) and regression (e.g., predicting housing prices).
  - Unsupervised Learning: Models learn from unlabeled data, finding hidden patterns. Common examples include clustering (e.g., customer segmentation) and dimensionality reduction.

Key Algorithms in Supervised Learning:

- Linear Regression: Used for predicting continuous variables. Learn how to fit a line to data points, the concept of the best fit, and the mean squared error for evaluating performance.
- Logistic Regression: Used for binary classification tasks (e.g., spam vs. not spam). Learn the sigmoid function and how it helps in decision-making.
- Decision Trees: A model that splits data into decision nodes based on feature values. Explore the concept of tree depth and pruning to prevent overfitting.

Key Algorithms in Unsupervised Learning:

- K-Means Clustering: Learn how to group data into clusters based on their similarities, and the concept of centroids and how clusters are formed.
- Principal Component Analysis (PCA): A dimensionality reduction technique that reduces the number of variables in the data while retaining the most important patterns.

Hands-on Practice:

- Practice Building Simple Models: Implement linear regression and k-means clustering using Scikit-Learn. Analyze the results and understand how algorithms learn from data.

Lesson 2: Feature Engineering

Data Cleaning:

- Handling Missing Data: Learn how to identify and manage missing data points. Techniques include filling missing values with the mean, median, or using more advanced methods like KNN imputation.
- Outlier Detection: Discover how to detect and remove outliers that can negatively impact model performance, using methods such as the Z-score and IQR (Interquartile Range).

Data Transformation:

- Encoding Categorical Variables: Convert categorical data (e.g., gender, location) into numerical formats that machine learning algorithms can understand. Learn one-hot encoding and label encoding.
- Creating New Features: Learn how to create new features from existing data that may improve model performance. For example, transforming date fields into features like "day of the week" or "is_weekend."

Feature Selection:

- Selecting Relevant Features: Not all features are helpful. Learn techniques like correlation analysis and feature importance from decision trees to identify which features contribute the most to the model's predictions.

- Removing Multicollinearity: Explore how highly correlated features can confuse a model and how to detect and address multicollinearity through techniques like Variance Inflation Factor (VIF).

Scaling and Normalizing Data:

- Standardization: Scale features to have a mean of 0 and a standard deviation of 1, ensuring that all features contribute equally to the model.
- Normalization: Transform features to a 0-1 range to ensure that no single feature dominates the model due to its scale.

Hands-on Practice:

- Data Preprocessing Exercises: Work with a dataset to clean, transform, and scale features. Build simple models before and after preprocessing to compare results.

Lesson 3: Advances Machine Learning Algorithms

Support Vector Machines (SVM):

- SVM Basics: Learn how Support Vector Machines create a hyperplane to separate classes in the data. Explore the concepts of support vectors and margins, and the importance of maximizing the margin to avoid overfitting.
- Kernels in SVM: Understand how kernels transform data into higher-dimensional space to handle complex, non-linear decision boundaries.

Ensemble Methods:

- Random Forests: A collection of decision trees that work together to improve model accuracy and stability. Learn how random forests reduce overfitting by averaging multiple trees trained on random subsets of data.
- Boosting Algorithms: Understand how boosting methods like AdaBoost and Gradient Boosting iteratively improve weak learners (e.g., shallow decision trees) by focusing on the most difficult data points.

Clustering and Dimensionality Reduction:

- Hierarchical Clustering: A clustering method that builds a hierarchy of clusters by recursively merging or

splitting them. Learn how dendrograms are used to visualize the clusters and choose the optimal number of clusters.
- t-SNE (t-Distributed Stochastic Neighbor Embedding): A dimensionality reduction technique used to visualize high-dimensional data in 2D or 3D space, often used for complex data like image or text features.

Hands-on Project:

- Classification Project: Implement a classification problem using Support Vector Machines and Random Forests. Compare the performance of these models using real-world data.
- Clustering Project: Use hierarchical clustering or t-SNE to analyze patterns in a high-dimensional dataset (e.g., customer segmentation).

Lesson 4: Model Evaluation and Optimization

Evaluating Classification Models:

- Confusion Matrix: A matrix used to evaluate the performance of classification models. Learn the concepts of True Positives, False Positives, True Negatives, and False Negatives.
- Evaluation Metrics
  - Accuracy: The proportion of correctly predicted labels.
  - Precision: The proportion of true positive predictions out of all positive predictions.
  - Recall: The proportion of true positives out of the actual positives.
  - F1 Score: The harmonic mean of precision and recall, useful when there is an imbalance in the data.

Evaluating Regression Models:

- Mean Absolute Error (MAE): The average absolute difference between predicted and actual values.
- Mean Squared Error (MSE): The average of the squares of the differences between predicted and actual values.
- R-Squared: A measure of how well the model fits the data. It represents the proportion of the variance in the dependent variable that is predictable from the independent variables.

Cross Validation:

- K-Fold Cross-Validation: A technique for assessing the generalization performance of a model by splitting the dataset into K equal parts, training the model on K-1 parts, and validating on the remaining part. This process is repeated K times, and the results are averaged.
- Stratified Cross-Validation: Ensure that each fold of the dataset has the same proportion of labels as the entire dataset, especially useful for imbalanced classification problems.

Hyperparameter Tuning:

- Grid Search: Systematically search for the best hyperparameters by testing all possible combinations of parameter values.
- Random Search: Randomly select hyperparameter values from the specified range, which can be more efficient for large search spaces.
- Bayesian Optimization: A more advanced method that uses probabilistic models to find the best hyperparameters based on previous results, rather than testing all combinations.

Deploying Machine Learning Models:

- Saving and Loading Models: Learn how to save trained models using joblib or pickle and load them for future predictions without retraining.
- Building APIs for Model Deployment: Use Flask or FastAPI to build simple web applications that serve

machine learning models as APIs, enabling real-time predictions.

Hands-On Project:

- Final Project: Apply cross-validation and hyperparameter tuning to a complex dataset (e.g., predicting house prices, sentiment analysis). Deploy the final model as an API and test its real-time performance.

MODULE 4

Data Science

Lesson 1: Introduction to Data Science

What is Data Science?

- Definition of Data Science: An interdisciplinary field that uses algorithms, data processing, and statistical methods to extract knowledge and insights from structured and unstructured data.
- Data Science Workflow
    - Data Collection: Gathering raw data from various sources (e.g., APIs, databases, web scraping).
    - Data Wrangling: Cleaning and preparing the data for analysis.
    - Exploratory Data Analysis (EDA): Summarizing and visualizing the data to discover patterns, spot anomalies, and check assumptions.
    - Modeling: Applying statistical models or machine learning algorithms to the data.
    - Communication: Presenting the insights and results using reports, visualizations, and storytelling.

Tools of the Trade:

- Python: The most popular language for data science due to its versatility and extensive libraries (Pandas, NumPy, Scikit-Learn).
- R: Another powerful tool for data analysis, particularly strong in statistical computing and visualization.

- SQL: Essential for querying and managing relational databases. Learn how to extract and manipulate data using SQL.
- Jupyter Notebooks: An interactive environment where data science code, visualizations, and explanations can be written and executed together.

Data Science in the Real World:

- Business Applications: How companies use data science for market analysis, customer segmentation, product recommendations, and fraud detection.
- Healthcare Applications: Predictive modeling for disease diagnosis, patient risk stratification, and personalized treatments.
- Government and Policy: Data-driven decision-making in policy formulation, public health management, and urban planning.

Hands-on Practice:

- Data Collection Exercise: Collect a dataset using an API or web scraping tool (e.g., collecting data on weather, finance, or social media trends).
- Introduction to SQL: Practice basic SQL queries to retrieve data from databases, join tables, and filter results.

Lesson 2: Data Visualization

The Importance of Data Visualization:

- Why Visualize Data?: Visualization helps in understanding complex data, spotting patterns, and communicating findings effectively to both technical and non-technical stakeholders.
- Types of Visualizations
    - Univariate Plots: Histograms, box plots, and bar charts for single variables.
    - Bivariate Plots: Scatter plots, heatmaps, and line charts to explore relationships between two variables.
    - Multivariate Plots: Pair plots, 3D scatter plots, and radar charts to show relationships between multiple variables.

Data Visualization Tools:

- Matplotlib: The foundation for creating static, animated, and interactive visualizations in Python. Learn to plot line graphs, bar charts, and scatter plots.
- Seaborn: Built on top of Matplotlib, Seaborn is designed for making complex statistical plots with simple commands. Learn to create heatmaps, violin plots, and pair plots.
- Plotly: A tool for creating interactive plots that can be shared on dashboards and websites. Learn to build interactive graphs such as zoomable line plots and choropleth maps.

- Tableau or Power BI: Learn to create professional dashboards for data storytelling and decision-making. These tools are widely used in business environments for their ability to integrate with databases and produce dynamic visualizations.

Data Storytelling:

- Choosing the Right Visualization: Learn how to select the appropriate chart type depending on the data and message (e.g., line charts for trends, pie charts for proportions).
- Narrative Flow: Create a coherent data story that guides the audience through the analysis step-by-step, highlighting the most critical insights.
- Avoiding Common Pitfalls: Recognize the dangers of misleading graphs, cherry-picked data, and data overload.

Hands-on Project:

- Visualization Project: Using a dataset (e.g., sales data, survey results, or social media data), create a set of visualizations that explore patterns and correlations. Present findings in a Jupyter notebook or Tableau dashboard.

Lesson 3: Statistical Analysis

Descriptive Statistics:

- Measures of Central Tendency: Learn how to calculate and interpret mean, median, and mode.
- Measures of Dispersion: Learn about variance, standard deviation, range, and interquartile range.
- Descriptive Statistics in Practice: Analyze datasets using Pandas to compute summary statistics, identify outliers, and understand the data distribution.

Inferential Statistics:

- Sampling and Population: Learn the concept of sampling and how to infer population characteristics from sample data.
- Hypothesis Testing:
  - Null and Alternative Hypotheses: Learn how to define hypotheses in the context of a research question.
  - P-values and Significance Levels: Understand how to interpret p-values and use them to make decisions.
  - T-tests and Chi-square Tests: Learn to apply common statistical tests to compare group means or proportions.

Probability Distributions:

- Normal Distribution: Learn about the bell curve and its importance in many real-world phenomena.
- Binomial and Poisson Distributions: Learn about discrete probability distributions commonly used in data science (e.g., in modeling rare events).
- Central Limit Theorem: Understand how sample means follow a normal distribution even if the population data is not normally distributed.

Advanced Statistical Concepts:

- Correlation and Causation: Learn to measure the strength of relationships between variables using correlation coefficients (e.g., Pearson, Spearman).
- Regression Analysis:
    - Simple Linear Regression: Understand how to model relationships between two variables and interpret regression coefficients.
    - Multiple Linear Regression: Explore more complex relationships involving multiple predictors, learning to evaluate model fit and multicollinearity.

Hands-on Practice:

- Statistical Analysis Project: Choose a dataset (e.g., social science survey data or economic data) and conduct an end-to-end statistical analysis. Interpret results, make inferences, and draw conclusions based on the data.

Lesson 4: Capstone Project

Project Selection:

- Dataset Selection: Choose a real-world dataset (e.g., from Kaggle, open government data, or company-provided data).
- Problem Definition: Clearly define a problem statement or research question that the project will address (e.g., predicting customer churn, analyzing climate data, or performing sentiment analysis on social media).

Exploratory Data Analysis (EDA):

- Data Wrangling: Clean the data by handling missing values, removing outliers, and transforming variables where necessary.
- Initial Insights: Use data visualization techniques to explore the data, uncover patterns, and generate hypotheses.

Modeling and Analysis:

- Model Building: Apply one or more statistical or machine learning models to the dataset. Examples include regression analysis, classification models, clustering, or time series forecasting.
- Model Evaluation: Use appropriate evaluation metrics to assess model performance (e.g., accuracy, RMSE, R-squared). Tune the model to optimize performance.

Data Visualization and Storytelling:

- Create Visualizations: Summarize the findings using visualizations that communicate the key insights effectively. Utilize dashboards if necessary for interactive exploration of the data.
- Narrative Presentation: Develop a narrative around the analysis. Explain the problem, approach, key findings, and recommendations in a clear, compelling manner.

Final Report:

- Write a Report: Summarize the entire project in a report that includes an introduction, methodology, analysis, results, and conclusion. This report should be clear enough to be understood by non-technical stakeholders

MODULE 5

Blockchain Technology

Lesson 1: What is Blockchain?

Blockchain Fundamentals:

- Definition of Blockchain: A decentralized, distributed ledger that records transactions across many computers in such a way that the records are secure, immutable, and transparent.
- How Blockchain Works
  - Blocks and Chains: Each block contains a number of transactions, a timestamp, and a cryptographic hash of the previous block, linking them in a chain.
  - Decentralization: No single entity controls the blockchain, which is maintained by multiple participants (nodes) in the network.
  - Consensus Mechanisms: Algorithms used to achieve agreement on a single data value or a single state of the network among distributed processes or systems (e.g., Proof of Work, Proof of Stake).

Blockchain Architecture:

- Key Components
  - Nodes: Devices participating in the network, maintaining copies of the blockchain.
  - Transactions: Actions initiated by participants that are recorded on the blockchain.
  - Miners/Validators: Participants who validate transactions and add them to the blockchain.

- Smart Contracts: Self-executing contracts where the terms are written into code. They automatically enforce and execute the terms of the agreement.
- Distributed Ledger Technology (DLT): Explains how DLT differs from traditional ledgers and why it is more secure and transparent.

Blockchain Use Cases:

- Cryptocurrencies: The most popular application of blockchain technology. Introduction to Bitcoin, Ethereum, and other cryptocurrencies.
- Supply Chain Management: Tracking the movement of goods and ensuring transparency.
- Healthcare: Securing medical records and patient data.
- Government Services: Voting systems, land registries, and identity verification.

Hands-on Practice:

- Exploring Block Explorers: Learn to navigate blockchain explorers like Etherscan to observe transactions, wallets, and smart contracts.

Lesson 2: Smart Contacts

Introduction to Smart Contracts:

- What are Smart Contracts?: Programs stored on the blockchain that execute when predefined conditions are met, enabling secure and automated transactions without intermediaries.
- Smart Contract Use Cases
    - DeFi (Decentralized Finance): Smart contracts enable lending, borrowing, trading, and earning interest without traditional banks.
    - NFTs (Non-Fungible Tokens): Smart contracts allow for the creation, sale, and transfer of unique digital assets, including art, collectibles, and gaming items.
    - Tokenization: Smart contracts facilitate the creation and management of digital tokens representing assets like stocks, real estate, or art.

Introduction to Solidity:

- Overview of Solidity: Solidity is the most widely used programming language for writing smart contracts on Ethereum. It is statically typed and supports inheritance, libraries, and complex user-defined types.
- Solidity Basics:
    - Syntax and Structure: Functions, state variables, and data types.
    - Modifiers: Enforce conditions on smart contract execution.
    - Events and Logs: Tracking and logging events in smart contracts.

- Smart Contract Lifecycle:
    - Deployment: Writing and deploying a smart contract on a blockchain.
    - Interaction: Calling contract functions and interacting with decentralized applications.

Hands-on Project:

- Building a Smart Contract: Create a basic smart contract (e.g., a simple escrow service or an NFT minting contract) using Solidity and deploy it on the Ethereum test network using tools like Remix IDE.
- Testing Smart Contracts: Use tools like Truffle or Hardhat to write and execute unit tests for the smart contract.

Lesson 3: Building Decentralized Applications (dApps)

What is a dApp?

- A decentralized application that operates on a blockchain rather than being hosted on centralized servers.
- Key Characteristics of dApps:
    - Decentralization: No single point of control or failure.
    - Open Source: The code is transparent and can be audited by anyone.
    - Incentivization: Often powered by tokens to encourage participation and decentralization.

dApp Architecture:

- Frontend: Typically built using web technologies like HTML, CSS, and JavaScript frameworks (e.g., React or Vue).
- Blockchain Backend: The core logic of the application is governed by smart contracts deployed on the blockchain.
- Wallet Integration: Wallets like MetaMask or WalletConnect are used to allow users to interact with the blockchain, sign transactions, and store digital assets.

Web3.js and Ether.js:

- Connecting dApps to the Blockchain: Learn to use Web3.js or Ether.js to interact with Ethereum smart contracts and blockchains from the frontend.
- Calling Smart Contract Functions: Learn to read from and write to the blockchain using functions like `sendTransaction()` and `call()`.
- Handling Blockchain Events: Learn how to listen for events emitted by smart contracts and update the dApp's frontend accordingly.

Hands-n Project:

- Building a Simple dApp: Build and deploy a decentralized voting system where users can vote on proposals. Users will be able to connect their wallets, cast votes, and see results updated in real-time. Deploy this dApp on the Ethereum test network.
- Testing and Deployment: Test the dApp on testnets like Ropsten or Rinkeby and deploy the final version to a mainnet (or testnet for student use).

Lesson 4: Blockchain Security and Future Trends

Blockchain Security:

- Common Vulnerabilities
    - Reentrancy Attacks: Exploit flaws in smart contracts where an external contract can repeatedly call back into the original contract.
    - Front-Running: Malicious actors observe pending transactions and execute their own transactions ahead of others to gain an advantage.
    - Private Key Management: The importance of securely managing private keys, as losing access to private keys means losing control of digital assets.
- Mitigating Security Risks
    - Smart Contract Audits: The process of reviewing smart contract code to identify and fix vulnerabilities before deployment.
    - Gas Limit Protection: Ensuring that smart contracts are designed to handle gas costs efficiently to prevent denial-of-service attacks.

    - Multi-Signature Wallets: Requiring multiple parties to approve transactions to prevent unauthorized access.

Layer 2 Solutions:

- Scaling Challenges: As blockchain adoption grows, scaling solutions are needed to increase transaction throughput and reduce fees on the network.
- Layer 2 Technologies
  - Rollups: Bundling many transactions into a single batch that is processed off-chain, reducing congestion on the main chain.
  - State Channels: Allowing participants to conduct transactions off-chain with only the final state being recorded on-chain, which reduces the burden on the network.
  - Plasma and Sidechains: Techniques for scaling by creating parallel chains that run alongside the main blockchain.

Future Trends in Blockchain:

- Interoperability: Bridging different blockchains to enable seamless communication and asset transfer between them.
- Decentralized Autonomous Organizations (DAOs): Organizations run by code, with decision-making automated by smart contracts and driven by token-holder votes.
- Privacy-Enhancing Technologies: The rise of privacy coins and privacy layers (e.g., ZK-SNARKs) to protect the anonymity of transactions on the blockchain.
- Web3 and the Decentralized Internet: Building a new decentralized web where users control their data and digital identities, with blockchain as the foundational technology.

Final Project:

- Develop a Full-Scale dApp: Students will create a larger project that integrates blockchain concepts learned throughout the module. Options could include a decentralized marketplace, a DeFi protocol, or a supply chain tracking system. The project will incorporate smart contracts, a frontend interface, and wallet integration. The final project will be deployed and tested on a blockchain network (testnet or mainnet depending on scale).

www.ingramcontent.com/pod-product-compliance
Lightning Source LLC
Chambersburg PA
CBHW070949220526
45471CB00007B/2962